T0365849

THE MERMAID LEGENDS:

Tales from the Watery Depths and the
Maidens of the Deep Blue Sea

BOOK 4

JAMES WHITMER

The Mermaid Legends: Tales from the Watery Depths and the Maidens of the Deep Blue Sea

BOOK 4

iUniverse books may be ordered through booksellers or by contacting:

iUniverse
1663 Liberty Drive
Bloomington, IN 47403
www.iuniverse.com
844-349-9409

ISBN: 978-1-6632-6909-6 (sc)
ISBN: 978-1-6632-6908-9 (e)

Library of Congress Control Number: 2024925032

Print information available on the last page.

iUniverse rev. date: 11/22/2024

Contents

The Beginning

#1a

Tales from the Watery Depths and the Maidens of the Deep Blue Sea

In deep sea depths no sailor's seen,
and under waves deep, bluish green,
the little mermaids gathered 'round,
a mermaid queen with a golden crown.

And in these watery depths this crown,
of ancient mermaid queens renowned,
of sirens from the deep blue seas,
who heard lost sailors' silent pleas,
this crown was handed neat, and slow,
just as these mermaids' eyes did glow,
and to an octopus deep green,
and in her eyes a scarlet sheen.

This octopus, her eyes did glisten,
her tentacles deep forest green,
as mermaids young and old did listen,
as did this lovely mermaid queen,
to tales she knew from ages past,
of clipper ships, their anchors cast,
in rolling, rocking seas of dread,
where squids did swim with purple heads,
through storms, and winds, and deep sea
squalls,
through sailors' songs and sailors' calls,
of fish with orange and yellow tails,
of tattered, torn, and windswept sails,
of silver slippers lost at sea,
of silver hair in midnight breeze,
of clipper ships and sturdy whalers,
of old sea cats and seasoned sailors,
of ships that sailed to far-off lands,
of cattails, tall, in colored sand,
of sailors clutching shipboard rails,
their faces hard as rusty nails,
of mermaids and their sailor's bands,
of mariners with sweet mermaid strands,
of seashells colored brown and tan,
and pirates with sharp hooks for hands,
of lighthouse beacons in the night,
of yellow birds in full-flung flight,
of doldrums thick with floating fishes,
of mermaids and their seamaid wishes,
of parrots in old crow's nests, high,
of crimson-coated, scarlet skies,

of common grackles dark as night,
of starlings, thick, in fancied flight,
of sea nymphs with deep, violet eyes,
that midnight clouds could not disguise,
of crocodiles with darkened snouts,
of pirates' jeers and pirates' shouts,
of butterflies upon the shore,
of anchors made of iron-ore,
of sailors' lanterns in the night,
and porpoises in circles, tight,
of pirate maps, both torn and old,
of sharks in waters deep and cold,
of rainbow fish, their colors bright,
of sailors lost and out of sight,
of chapels where bronze bells did ring,
where sailors' daughters prayed, did sing,
when ships from far-off, distant lands,
their anchors cast near friendly sands,
and rain as dark as midnight thunder,
of sea swells swirling deep down under,
of waves from raging tempests, dark,
and pirates' eyes as black as sharks',
of glittering, Spanish sparkling gold,
of mariners' stories new and old,
of beaches glowing like the sun,
of mermaids' hair, bright, long, undone,
and flowing free in sea-salt breeze,
as mariners' daughters, on their knees,
and clutching mariners' rosaries,
did pray aloud for their return,
as wind and waves and waters churned,
so far away, near distant lands,
away from surf and friendly sands.

These mermaids, each and every one,
did take these stories, legends, old,
to aid these sailors brave and bold,
into the silence of the seas,
to seek these sailors' silent pleas,
and swim to far-off, distant shores,
where wind and sleet and rain does pour,
and then return to friendly sands,
and daughters with their outstretched hands,
these maidens of the mainland who,
do scan and scan the oceans blue.

The Mermaid *Lorelei* and Her Song of the Sea

The lovely mermaid, *Lorelei*,
a seamaid from the seven seas,
a siren from the watery depths,
swimming slow, she holds her breath.

A water nymph with deep, red curls,
that glimmer, glow, in soft sea swirls,
she swims along a shoreline, bright,
where rockfish gather in the night.

And as she swims she sings her song,
and as the other seamaids listen,
and as her eyes search far and wide,
her deep, red fins, they glimmer, glisten.

Her golden eyes like shooting stars,
into the deep, dark nights are glowing.
Her chants like gently strummed guitars,
they hum across the sandbars, flowing.

So, *Lorelei*'s song of the sea,
it holds a long-lost mystery,
through circling waves and oceans, blue,
about a sailor she once knew.

He sailed the oceans far and wide,
and with his sea cat at his side,
he wore her strand of deep, red hair,
around his neck with love and care,
but in the swirling, churning seas,
he was lost for evermore,
and now she seeks his long-lost pleas,
and prays to see him as before.

So, as her lovely siren song,
does whisper to the waters, clear,
does waft across the starfish sleeping,
and where red frogs and toads are leaping,
across this beach that moonbeams cloak,
across this beach blue waves do soak,
the silent, listening, other maids,
sweet maids her siren song does kiss,
sweet prayers upon their seamaid lips,
they swim to moonlight ever streaming,
with *Lorelei,* as she is dreaming,
about this sailor lost at sea,
her heart forever slowly beating,
that he will hear her desperate plea.

The Mermaid *Belladonna* and the Sea Before the Storm

Before dark tempests in the night,
above the dwindling, golden light,
form deep, loud thunder in the skies,
the mermaid *Belladonna's* eyes,
they glow and glimmer, as she waits,
with angelfish along her side.
Her palms across the waves do glide.

As twilight makes its presence known,
the mermaid *Belladonna* swims,
quite silently and all alone,
the winds serene and ever calm,
the thunder patient like a psalm,
no lightning in the skies above,
just peacefulness, like wings of doves.

But when the angelfish do swim,
in circles growing ever small,
the heavens crash. The skies turn purple,
and *Belladonna* sounds the call,
to creatures of the cold, dark deep,
to birds above the waters, steep,
to otters resting in the weeds,
to harbor seals among the reeds,
to starfish in the rushes, all,
to frogs and toads in cattails, tall.

So, to her maiden song they listen,
and patiently they heed her call,
and as the skies turn dark as coal,
and as the swelling sea does roll,
they scatter to the safety of,
the rocks and ledges and the caves,
and out of sight and ever deep,
far from the ever-crashing waves.

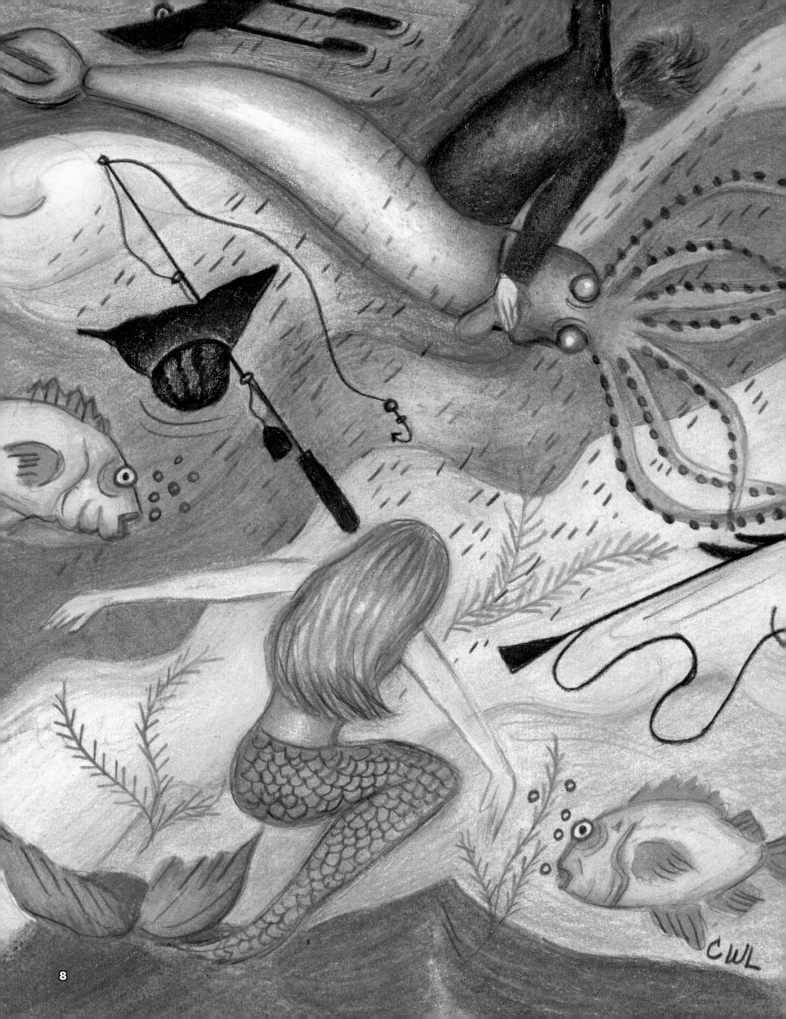

The Mermaid *Aquata* and the Lonesome Fisherman

He sat alone in a boat too small,
in a rolling, rocking, deep sea squall.
The mermaid *Aquata*, swimming nearby,
cast her eyes to the water and then to the sky.

His eyes were the color of dark midnight skies,
as salt water dripped from old sailor's eyes.
He let out a call, then looked out to the sea,
and saw sweet *Aquata* swimming fancy and free.

So, she sang her sweet ode and a squid did arise,
from the watery depths with sparkling blue eyes.
Its eyes were like sapphires that glimmered and glowed.
Its head was deep purple, as the fisherman rowed.

Then it did what this lovely sea maiden had taught it,
and it swam toward the rowboat adrift in the sea.
With tentacles purple, like deep-blooming orchids,
it grasped this old mariner, steadfast and free.

And then to the mainland this sailor did ride,
on the back of this squid and toward friendly tides,
with the mermaid *Aquata,* and her free-flowing hair,
singing low her sweet ode in the soft sea-salt air.

The Mermaid *Arabella* and the
Waterfall of a Different Color

Her yellow hair above the waves,
her eyes like golden sunsets streaming,
she swims in silent, hidden waters,
white moonlight on the waters gleaming.

Under waterfalls deep blue,
live sea birds with a velvet hue,
their nests among the starfish sleeping,
among the red crabs slowly creeping.

But in the midnight shadows looming,
among the silver lilies blooming,
this waterfall of deepest blue,
assumes a crimson, scarlet hue.

And underneath deep shades of red,
where red crabs nested, swam, and fed,
the waters bubbled, churned, and glowed,
and where red eels, they lived below,
in watery depths no sailor knew,
they guarded shiny pearls, deep blue.

Sweet *Arabella* knows this legend,
and where these turquoise pearls do rest,
and guarded by these eels, deep red,
inside a sunken treasure chest.

So, to this chest this seamaid swam,
to find these sparkling turquoise stones,
and soon to rest in mermaids' strands,
where sea queens sit on mermaid thrones,
and to these dark red eels she sang,
her sea nymph song from ages past,
and to the waves these eels did swim,
into blue oceans far and vast.

The Mermaid *Breena* and the Purple Lilies

In the darkness of the evening,
and when the fireflies' glow is low,
sweet *Breena,* with her fins deep purple,
she swims in waters ever slow.

Her hair like scarlet, shades of twilight,
and when the moon is looming low,
and in the shadows of the moonlight,
her deep red braids are all aglow.

In her heart she holds a legend,
of long ago and sunsets past,
of deep blue seas and ivory beaches,
of lilies growing neat and fast.

This legend tells of sandbars glowing,
with golden sand, both neat and bright.
It tells of purple lilies growing,
into the deep, dark, velvet night.

So, underneath the fireflies' glow,
as crickets sing in voices, low,
along this sandbar shining bright,
with stars above in deep, dark night,
these purple lilies, they do grow,
pure and perfect, row by row.

And as this mermaid legend said,
a firefly of the deepest gold,
it would alight upon a lily,
and fulfill this legend old.

So, in the midnight's looming shadows,
and underneath this firefly's glow,
sweet *Breena,* with her braided hair,
does pluck this lily ever slow.

And underneath this purple lily,
a turquoise gemstone neatly rests,
and once worn by a mermaid queen,
in mermaid crowns and mermaid crests.

So, with this gem from sunsets past,
and lost among the purple lilies,
to the mainland *Breena* glides,
a golden stingray by her side.

With golden fireflies in her hair,
and swimming slow, this maiden, fair,
this sea nymph from the seven seas,
this seamaid gliding free, at ease,
she clutches to her breast this prize,
a firefly's glimmer in her eyes.

14

#6
The Mermaid *Caspia*: The Seamaid with the Violet Eyes

Along a shore where seabirds nest,
among palm trees where toucans rest,
a mermaid with her colors bright,
swims under sparkling, gold moonlight.

A moon does glow with golden shades,
and as the twinkling starlight fades,
she scans the shore with violet eyes.
Their beauty night cannot disguise.

So, in the midnight shadows looming,
gold lilies on the shoreline blooming,
a toucan of the brightest colors,
does call to her and nestles low,
among the lilies' vibrant glow.

Then with her sparkling violet eyes,
in midnight shadows she does spy,
a single, lonesome lily, gold,
just as the mermaid legend told.

Inside its petals, opening free,
does rest a pearl long lost at sea.

This pearl was worn by mariner kings,
and then was found in wizards' rings,
sea wizards of the surf and sand,
with powers over sea and land,
but now this shining, long-lost prize,
does glow as bright as violet eyes,
and so sweet *Caspia* swims away,
to where sea lions dance and play.

The Mermaid *Sweet Nixie* and the Ten Little Starfish

Ten little mermaids, all in a row,
ten little mermaids, eyes all aglow,
they rode on seahorses in warm ocean swirls,
and all had long hair, and bright golden curls.

They swam in tight circles in yellow moonlight.
Their fins were the color of yellow sunlight.
Ten little mermaids were followed quite slow,
by ten little starfish, their colors aglow.

These starfish were red, blue, green, and deep black,
with a streak of deep yellow adorning their backs.
As *Sweet Nixie* sang her sweet mermaid ode,
on ten spunky seahorses, these seamaids, they rode.

They rode in tight circles, these ten little maids,
and under soft moonlight in soft moonlight shades,
and each with a starfish aglow in the night,
as *Sweet Nixie* hummed, so soft with delight.

And when they were done and the sun did arise,
these ten little seamaids withs stars in their eyes,
they rode to warm waters where palm trees did sway,
as ten little starfish continued to play.

The Mermaid *Myranda* and the Red Sea Witch

Upon an island deep with palms,
its beaches thick with colored sand,
lived a witch who ruled the seas,
with power over surf and land.

This witch was once a mermaid queen,
with angel hair and glowing bangs,
but in the darkness of the depths,
and bitten by deep sea snakes' fangs,
she casts her spells across the waves,
into the dark, forbidden caves.

So, now her hair is lava red,
her fins aflame with fiery flames,
a deep red star upon her head,
and *Schorcha* is her sea witch name.

And by this island flush with palms,
sea maidens never swam,
but then one day a maid did land,
upon this colored sand.

She knew the legends of this witch,
the stories through and true.
Just as the swirling sea did pitch,
she placed a kiss upon her lips.
Her eyes turned turquoise blue.

Her fins a deep and fiery red,
now had a deep sea hue.
The crimson star upon her head
glowed with a velvet blue.

Her hair turned white as angels' hair,
her tears were ever true.
She kissed *Myranda* on her cheek,
her smile serene and ever meek,
then swam to oceans blue.

So, sweet *Myranda* saved this queen,
from clutches dark and deep.
Forever more the mermaids, fair,
this legend, they will keep.

20

#9
The Mermaid *Layke* and the Pirate on the Beach

An old sea cat on rocky sand,
it sleeps at the feet where a pirate stands,
on a bright, white beach where seagulls nest,
where a stealthy pirate seeks a treasure chest.

One eye is green, the other blue.
She glides with strokes both tried and true.
Sweet *Layke,* with her flowing hair,
she swims in gentle, sea-salt air,
along this narrow, rocky beach,
a treasure chest within her reach.

This pirate with his old spyglass,
and with his sea horn made of brass,
does search the shoreline far and wide,
and with his sea cat by his side,
he sees sweet *Layke* as she glides,
splashing waves from side to side.

This pirate with his braids of red,
a black bandana 'round his head,
a golden cross hung from each ear,
across his face, this buccaneer,
no smile, but just a pirate's sneer.

Sweet *Layke* knows this mermaid legend,
of where a pirate's chest does lie.
She chants her ode and calls their names.
Their flapping fins soon fill the sky.

In moments they are there in swirls,
these flying fish all colored bright.
They flap their fins so ever fast.
This pirate flees into the night.

So, on this rocky, narrow beach,
this old sea cat, it did remain,
and with its purring low and sweet,
purred out a gentle, soft refrain.

It sleeps above a sanded crest,
below which lies a treasure chest,
that's filled with coins and silver rings,
and gold doubloons and shiny things.

The Mermaid *Sharena* and the Albatross with the Silver Tail

In his eyes, a pirate's stare,
and in the wind, his eyes did flare,
just as a silver-tailed bird,
did perch upon the mizzenmast.

Onto the deck, its eyes were cast,
onto this pirate, eyes deep dark,
and where a shark had left its mark,
upon a hardened pirate's face,
around his neck a scarf of lace,
a golden tooth that glowed and gleamed,
and when he spoke it almost seemed,
the swelling ocean rocked and shook,
and for one hand a sailor's hook.

Sharena swam around his ship,
her lovely finger on her lip,
and sang in sweet and gentle tones,
but to this silver-tailed bird,
she uttered not a single word.

Her hair was flowing rich and long,
and colored bright as heavens, clear,
and as she sang her seamaid song,
a golden earring in each ear,
this silver-tailed albatross,
did fly to her with wings outspread,
a silver star upon its head.

And as the ancient legend told,
this bird of blue would lead to gold,
lost from a sailing ship of old,
in rolling waters deep and cold.

This pirate ship did sway and rock,
its anchor cast into the shallows.
This pirate with his yellowed eyes,
as dark as burning candles' tallow,
strained to see this bird of blue,
but in his heart, he truly knew,
to where this bird would finally rest.
His sails unfurled, his anchor up,
into the sun, he headed west.

24

CWL

The Mermaid *Havilah*: The Seamaid and the Golden Sunset

A golden sunset on the shore,
a colored moon shines high above.
Her eyes are soft with heaven's glow.
Sweet *Havilah* seeks her sailor love.

His ship is coming into sight.
Bright stars are dancing in the night.
She glides in waters clear but cold,
sings out her lovely seamaid ode.

And as his ship sails into shore,
he tosses her a ring of gold.
It sparkles bright with glowing diamonds,
deep from the many thousand islands.

This ring she places on her finger.
A strand of dark and scarlet hair,
is flung to him with words unsaid,
her sweet ode floating in the air.

This sailor, with his sailor's stare,
and with his wind-blown, sailor's hair,
he listens close. Her waves do splash,
and as his sailor's eyes do flash,
her lovely mermaid melody,
does float across the open sea.

Then from his schooner's polished deck,
her strand of hair around his neck,
his eyes now filled with love and bliss,
he blows to her a sailor's kiss,
and from his windburned, sailor's lips,
and from his old, seaworthy ship.

#12
The Mermaid *Merrow* and the Two Lost Schooners

Two schooners sailed straight out to sea,
one blustery, wind-filled, autumn day.
The mariner in the lighthouse watched.
Through whitecaps, high, they made their way.

But that was months and months ago,
and so this mariner knew,
these sailing ships, both sleek and trim,
were lost in oceans blue.

Around his lighthouse *Merrow* swam,
through morning fog to setting sun,
her eyes fixed on the swirling tides,
and ever-changing, deep blue skies.

Then calling out her maiden name,
sweet *Merrow*, from his windowpane,
he bid her find theses schooners, lost,
in darkened seas, horizons crossed,
in unknown storms and sleet and rain,
while in the lighthouse, he remained.

Sweet *Merrow,* with her auburn hair,
and deep red fins to match,
whistled low and waved good-bye.
The mariner closed the hatch.

Days and days passed endlessly,
this mariner looking out to sea,
but then one day in winter's frost,
Merrow and two schooners, lost,
the far horizon, they did cross,
into a shadowy, dark midnight,
a rolling whitecap not in sight.

The Sea Maiden *Iora* and the Shark with the Emerald Eyes

In the oceans far and wide,
live sharks with slashing, gray-white tails,
but only one has emerald eyes,
and teeth as strong as iron nails.

Pirates, sailors, mariners, all,
have searched the rolling, rocking seas,
to find this shark with emerald eyes,
for long ago, it swallowed a key.

This key the ancient legend tells,
will fit a hidden pirate's chest,
lost long ago in desperate seas,
among lost sailors' silent pleas,
and sealed tight with a mermaid's crest.

This mermaid's crest is made of gold,
or so the ancient legend told,
and of a mermaid queen of old,
and given from a sailor, bold.

This legend sweet *Iora* knows,
about this crest of sparkling gold,
was worn when sharks did rule the seas,
'round sunken ships and sailors' pleas.

And now this emerald key does rest,
inside a mouth with iron teeth.
So, to this shark *Iora* swims,
around her neck a sailor's wreath.

Emerald-eyed and swimming slow,
along a beach *Iora* knows,
these emerald eyes did flash and glow,
just as *Iora,* she did throw,
from 'round her neck this sailor's wreath,
and it was caught by iron teeth.
The emerald key within its mouth,
spit out just like a waterspout.

So, to this key *Iora* swam,
while singing loud her maiden ode,
in waters clear but ever cold,
just as this shark with iron teeth,
did swim along an emerald reef,
with eyes that blinked so ever brief.

So, with this key in mermaid hands,
she swam back to the reeds and sands,
and placed this emerald, sparkling key,
flush at a place where it should be,
within the dainty, thankful hands,
a maiden of the reeds and sands.

This maiden is the daughter of,
a sailor lost in swirling storms.
Around his neck he wore this key,
through winters cold and summers warm,
and now it rests where it should be,
and from a maiden of the sea,
a sea nymph swimming fast and free.

This pirate chest this key will fit,
rests near a chapel on the shore,
and when its bells do ring and clang,
and when its sea-chimes clink and bang,
they're ringing out *Iora's* name,
forever clear, forever more,
this sailors' chapel on the shore.

The Mermaid *Lana* and the Old Pirate's Map

A common grackle on each arm,
ten starlings on the mizzenmast,
this pirate in his pirate ship,
his anchor to the sea was cast.

A copper spyglass on his hip,
he scanned the waters from his ship,
in one hand a pirate's map,
and on his head an old sea cap.

The mermaid *Lana*, on the beach,
she saw this ship within her reach.
She knew the legend though and true,
and what this pirate just might do.

She sang her lovely mermaid tune,
across the sandbars and the dunes.
In seconds they were there in pairs,
with flashing eyes like fiery flares.

These flying fish of different colors,
swooned, and dipped, and filled the skies.
Then to this pirate ship they flew,
as *Lana* swam in waters, blue.

This pirate on his rocking deck,
a gold medallion 'round his neck,
an old rope snug around his waist,
a pirate's sneer across his face,
a skull-and-crossbones waving free,
above the blue-gray, rolling sea,
did try to wave these fish away.
The starlings up above just swayed.

These grackles with their deep, black beaks,
their wings adorned with deep, black streaks,
then plucked this map from stealthy hands,
and fast they flew to reeds and sands.

And then the starlings up above,
they followed close these flying fish,
and drove this pirate ship away,
then followed for a night and day.

So, *Lana*, with her eyes deep black,
just like the streaks on grackles' backs,
retrieved this old and wrinkled map,
a common grackle on her lap.

The Mermaid *Starista* and The Red Admiral Butterflies

Its middle dark and deep coal-black,
its wings are streaked with fire.
It spreads them in the sky above,
like children chanting in a choir.

In full-flung flight red melds with black.
Its wings are tipped with white.
Some brownish tints are on its back,
but hard to see in fancied flight.

An *Admiral*, yes, that is its name,
with red its flashing color,
but black remains upon its back,
a midnight cloak appearing duller.

And when they're seen above the fields,
and resting neat in stalks of corn,
the children marvel at their colors,
in afternoons and early morns.

And sweet *Starista* knows these colors,
and knows them through and true,
and when her sailor love's sleek schooner,
through the fog and morning dew,
does make its way to shore and sand,
she wears his bold, red sailor's band,
around her waist, cinched ever tight,
and sees its name in letters, bright,
and to her heart a welcome sight.

Across its weathered, wood-worn stern,
in seaman's script both bold and clear,
in colors deep, like butterfly wings,
its name *Red Admiral* does appear.

And as she sits upon the shore,
Red Admirals on her lap,
her sailor love from voyages past,
he blows a kiss and tips his hat.

The Mermaid *Sesquanna* and the Thousand Islands

Among vast oceans far and wide,
among the rolling, frothing tides,
there lives a maiden of the sea,
who swims alone and ever free.

Her hair is braided, turquoise blue.
Her fins are of a purple hue.
Her slender frame is trim and sleek.
A rosy gloss adorns each cheek.

Among the many thousand islands,
is where you'll find this lovely maid,
who lives among the reefs and sands,
a seamaid holding in her hands,
a sailor's cross of sparkling gold,
and lost in waters deep and cold.

So, now she swims among these islands,
her eyes like Spanish, sparkling diamonds,
and like the earrings she now wears,
that sparkle like her turquoise hair.

One moonswept night long, long ago,
and on a beach where moonbeams glowed,
these sparkling earrings were a gift,
and from a sailor brave and true,
and to a nymph, hair turquoise blue.

Sesquana is her maiden name.
She's known for deep sea diving fame,
and that is how she found his cross,
and as the rolling waves did toss,
in seas as dark as midnight thunder,
in gloomy waters, deep down under.

But that was months and months ago.
So, now she waits among these islands,
searching long across the waves,
with eyes like Spanish, sparkling diamonds.

She prays to see his long-lost ship,
returning from a sailing trip,
to dock near friendly, pebbled sand,
his sailor's cross held in her hand.

The Mermaid *Romina*: The Seamaid with the Crimson Eyes

Her eyes like sunsets, crimson bright,
they glow like embers in the night.
When seen from ships on open seas,
they beckon sailors fast and free,
to sail to her, and hear her song,
in dazzling moonlight, lingering long.

Her eyes do soothe. They hypnotize,
bring tears to seasoned sailors' eyes,
but only one *Romina* seeks,
who sailed waves with enormous peaks,
through whitecaps large as whales' backs.
No stiff resolve this sailor lacked.

And so she swims in bright moonlight,
and sings her song throughout the night,
and waits and listens for his ship,
a seamaid's kiss upon her lips.

Through winters, dark, and summers, long,
she sings her lovely seamaid song.
Her dancing, crimson globes for eyes,
foretell a love night can't disguise.

And then one day in early spring,
the sun, a new day it did bring,
and on the distant ocean line,
perfect, neat, forever fine,
she saw him steering at the helm,
and making way through sea swells, steep,
just as her crimson eyes did flash,
a promise in his heart he keeps.

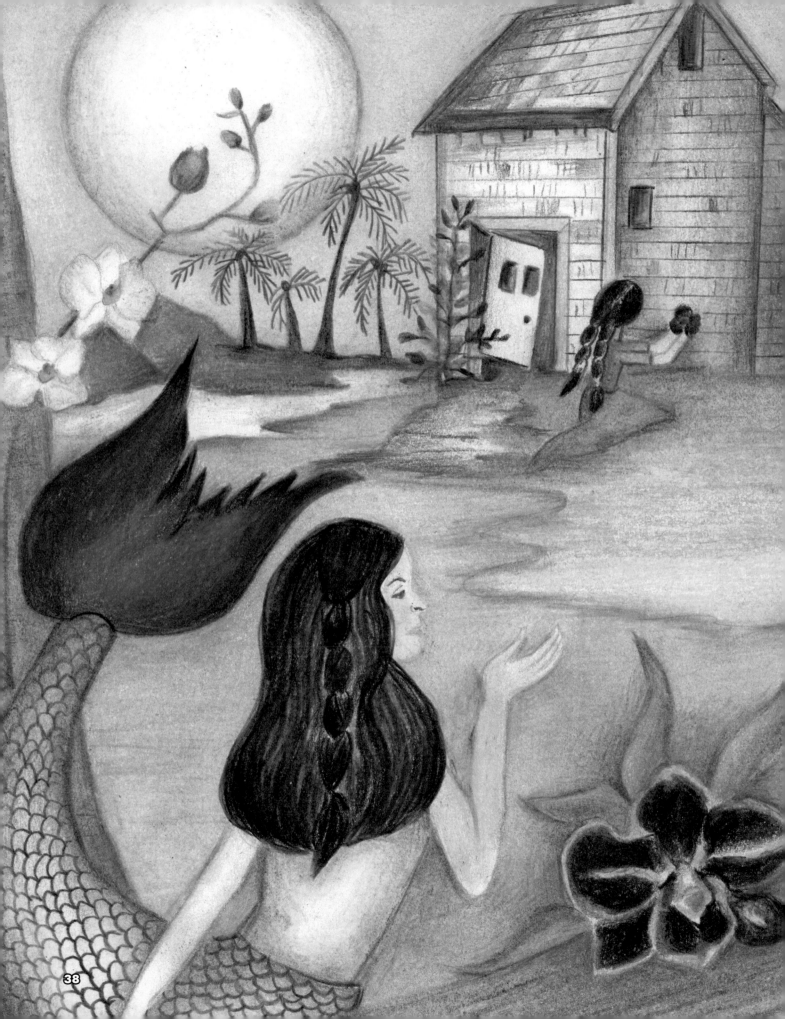

18

The Mermaid *Nori* and the Black Orchid

A purple moon above did shine,
upon a purple shore.
A deep, black orchid, dark as night,
grew near an open door.

This door led to a mariner's shack,
where lived a lovely maid,
above a beach where orchids grew,
and where this maid did play.

These orchids on the sandy beach,
were white as fallen snow,
but this orchid at her door,
black petals, it did grow.

This deep, black orchid once a gift,
a sea nymph to a sailor, bold,
sweet *Nori* gave her sailor love,
just like the mermaid legend told.

Upon an island thick with palms,
this orchid, it once grew,
upon a beach with purple fronds,
that only mermaids knew.

And when she wore it in her hair,
it matched her lovely braids,
and when they met upon the shore,
a gift to him was made.

But he was lost in winter storms,
his daughter now alone,
and near a shack with ivy vines,
this orchid, it is grown.

It blossoms neat in moonlight shadows,
and underneath a purple moon,
but only when sweet *Nori* sings,
her lovely, soothing, seamaid tune.

So, at her door this orchid grows,
when purple moonlight shines,
just as this maid caresses petals,
next to a shack with ivy vines.

And when sweet *Nori* sings her song,
into the violet-shaded night,
sweet, sublime and lasting long,
this orchid is a wondrous sight.

19

The Sea Nymph *Capri* and the Red Eagle

An eagle soars above the water,
while on the shore, a mariner's daughter,
she waits with patient, praying hands,
among the swaying reeds and sands,
a mariner's rosary in her hands.

Below is swimming sweet *Capri*,
a seamaid swimming fast and free.
Along this beach, she skims the waves,
above deep, dark, and hidden caves.

She sees this eagle flying high.
Deep red its colors, like its eyes,
that flash like night fires burning bright,
like torches glowing through the night.

Sweet *Capri,* she knows this maiden,
this tender maid who waits on shore,
who seeks her father lost at sea,
a sailor lost in deep, dark storms.

And sweet *Capri*, she knows this legend,
and how to find his missing ship.
So, to her mouth she clasps her hands.
Sweet music flows from mermaid lips.

This eagle high above the shore,
it hears this seamaid's soothing call,
then skims the waves near where she swims,
then as the fading sun does fall,
flies to a place where sea meets sky,
and flashes bright its eagle's eyes.

Sweet *Capri*, her duty done,
she swims to waves just where the sun,
does dip below the gray-white waters,
and left on shore, this mariner's daughter.

Days and days pass slowly by.
This sailor's daughter scans the sky,
then sees this deep red flying bird,
and then a ship, then shouts are heard.

And as the seamaid legend said,
a ship led by a bird of red,
it will return from desperate seas,
as daughters pray on desperate knees.

Flush across this ship's stout bow,
its name replete in letters bold,
Red Eagle is her sailing name,
just like the ancient legend told.

20

The Mermaid *Cordelia*: The Sea Nymph with the Silver Eyes

A young sailor looked straight out to sea,
from the stern of his whaling ship,
and he saw a young mermaid swimming free,
with a ruby-red glow to her lips.

He bid her to swim to the stern of his ship.
He yearned for a better look,
but a pirate appeared in a pirate ship.
One hand was a golden hook.

But her bright silver eyes did cast a glow,
across the silent waves.
This sailor's stare, it hung in the air,
above the deep sea caves.

But sweet *Cordelia,* swimming slow,
with hair like her silver eyes,
swam close to this deep sea, whaling ship,
and away from the darkening skies.

Her hair had a deep sea ocean tint,
that glowed with a silver hue.
Her fins the color of sparkling rubies,
glowed bright in the deep sea, blue.

This pirate with dark and braided hair,
sailed ever so near to this sea nymph, fair.
His hook for a hand was dark like the sky.
His target was the maid with the silver eyes.

But the darkening skies
were black, indeed,
and fast approaching his ship.

The waves were fast,
and covered with foam,
and rolled at an even clip.

But the wind picked up,
the sails unfurled,
on his sea-worthy whaling ship.

And seabirds appeared,
as a mermaid song,
was sung from sweet mermaid lips.

With fast-flapping wings that filled the sky,
this pirate was forced away.
This silver-eyed nymph then whistled again,
and dolphins began to play.

Both white and gray, dark streaks on their breasts,
they forced this pirate away to the west,
as the red, setting sun, it began to fade,
a sleek crimson shadow and neatly displayed,
as her silver eyes glowed, and she held her breath,
as she glided so neat over deep sea depths,
while this sailor alone, at the stern of his ship,
blew a kiss, then touched his wind-burned lips.

Then to this lovely, silver-eyed nymph,
he threw high in the air his sailor's band,
from the stern of his sea-worthy whaling ship.
She caught it, then placed it flush on her hand.

She then blew a kiss back where he did stand,
on the stern of his sea-worthy whaling ship,
then sang her sweet song while clutching his band,
a silver-eyed nymph with a kiss on her lips.

21

The Mermaid *Enya* and the Midnight Pirate

Under painted pirate curls,
his ship adrift in ocean swirls,
his eyes a deepened midnight black,
a coal-black cape upon his back,
this pirate with his moustache, dark,
his eyes as stealthy as a shark's,
was born in midnight's gloomy shadows,
upon a ship docked in the shallows.

This midnight pirate scanned the shore,
along a beach where *Enya* swam,
his spyglass steady in his hand,
sweet *Enya*'s eyes like polished sand,
and swimming free like sirens do,
in waters clear and vibrant blue,
he wished he knew what *Enya* knew.

The legend of a long-lost ship,
lost on a long-lost sailing trip,
that carried treasures from the East,
when rain from dark skies was released,
was lost among the thousand islands,
where lived the many mermaid sirens.

Sweet *Enya* knows this mermaid legend,
and where this sailing ship was lost.
It carried treasures of a king,
gold and silver, bracelets, rings,
and lots of other shiny things,
and lost at midnight in a storm,
in waters churning, dark but warm.

So, *Enya* waits for moonbeams streaming,
to mark the spot on waters gleaming,
where she will dive with other sirens,
below the fading, dark horizon.

But with his spyglass at his side,
this pirate scanned the waters wide.
His eyes were sharp, his stare severe,
his anchor cast, sweet *Enya* near.

Sweet *Enya* swimming neat and slow,
her eyes afire and aglow,
and with her vibrant mermaid chant,
that did entice and did enchant,
she summoned shoals of blue-black sharks,
their shiny eyes, pinpoint, and dark.

Around this pirate ship they swam,
and with their snouts just like a ram,
they forced this pirate ship away.
Into the wind, its sails did sway,
then followed for a night and day.

So, with this midnight pirate gone,
and with the moonbeams on the waves,
sweet *Enya* and her sister sirens,
they dove to deep and hidden caves,
to find this treasure lost at sea,
then swam to waves where they should be.

22

The Mermaid *Sedna* and the Sea Wizard's Ring

The sea wizard's hair was white as bright snow,
but his teeth were as dark as coal.
He lived near a beach where dolphins swam,
in shoal, after shoal, after shoal.

These dolphins were red from a spell he had cast,
in the waters around this beach.
His potions were bright and glowed in the night,
and were always within his reach.

The sweet mermaid *Sedna* had violet hair,
and violet eyes to match.
She swam to the beach where this old wizard
lived,
with a chest with a silver latch.

No one knew how to open this chest,
not a mermaid queen, nor a king.
So, she swam to this wizard with potions, bright.
On his finger was a wizard's ring.

She swam to a rock on the pebbled, white sand,
with her fins dangling fancy and free.
She sat on this rock, then waved her sweet hand,
at a place only mermaids could see.

Then she sang her sweet song in the soft,
sea-salt air,
a melody born of the night.
Red dolphins appeared and swimming in pairs.
Their colors were scarlet and bright.

Above the calm sea, their heads in a row,
they bobbed up and down,
as sweet music flowed,
from the lips of sweet *Sedna*,
as the wizard came close,
with a curious look, as he twitched his old nose.

"*I see you have magic*," the sea wizard said.
Sweet *Sedna,* she listened, then nodded her
head.
"*Except for this problem*." She showed him the
chest,
patted it softly, then held her sweet breath.

"*I see*," said the wizard, his hand in the air,
and then with his ring, with fervor and flair,
a bolt of red lightning hit flush on the latch.
It opened just slightly. Her eyes, they did catch,
a glimmer of glee in wizened, old eyes,
as he looked at the chest, then deeply inside.

Inside was a ring, like the one on his hand,
with power over islands, oceans, and sand.
This ring he then gave to this sea maiden, fair,
cast a spell to the waters, then into the air.

The dolphins turned gray, their natural color.
Then into the air, and holding his collar,
he vanished from sight from this sandy, white
beach,
in a burst of bright light, as the legend did teach.

So, the seamaid, sweet *Sedna*,
with a sea wizard's ring,
swam back to the dolphins. These dolphins did
sing,
in tune with the song from a lovely seamaid,
as the orangish-red sun over waves, it did fade.

23

The Mermaid *Delia* and the Unicorn with the Golden Eyes

A unicorn roamed,
on a sundrenched beach,
with a tail as gold as the sand.

A mermaid swam,
along this beach,
with her hair in golden strands.

The unicorn's tail,
was gold, indeed,
and it matched the unicorn's eyes.

But the sea nymph swimming
with golden strands,
had eyes as blue as the sky.

And then one day when a fog cloaked this beach,
a fog as gold as the sun,
this unicorn galloped to this mermaid, fair,
with her bright, golden hair undone.

On his back was a bird with a golden key,
and it flew to her waiting lap,
cooed ever so softly, then flew straight away.
On her lap this golden key did stay,
as the unicorn whinnied, then galloped away.

But *Delia* knew not,
what this gold key would fit.
Some treasure she thought,
she did quite admit.

So, back into the waves,
she returned in a flash,
and as these deep waves,
they did heave and did crash,
she would seek the advice
of the mermaid queens, three,
who ruled over oceans,
sandbars, and seas.

24

The Mermaid *Delia*, The Golden Key, and the Mermaid Queens, Three

Some folks say in the watery depths
a chest lies deep in the sand,
and it takes four keys to open it up,
by a seamaid with golden strands.

The mermaid queens, three,
they all knew this legend,
and where in the sand to search,
deep under the waves that are purple and gray,
and near an old mariner's church.

So, with these three keys,
from the mermaid queens, three,
sweet *Delia* swam to the shore,
where an old sailor's church,
on a rock ledge did lurch,
with a maiden alone at the door.

This maiden had hair,
as gold as the sun,
and a starfish within her hand.

"He'll take you right there,"
her voice sweet in the air,
"And down to the ivory sand."

Then she pointed with flair,
where a cross it did stand,
on a sandbar with ivory sand,
and that's where she'd dive,
with four golden keys,
and a starfish within her sweet hands.

This maiden on shore,
knew a chest there did lie,
under waves and silky, white foam.

So, she waited on shore,
near an old sailor's door,
near the treasure that was her sweet home.

25

The Mermaid *Serenia* and the Sapphire Shore

The mermaid *Serenia,*
had dark, silken hair,
and beautiful sapphire eyes.

She lived near a beach,
where palm trees grew tall,
reaching into the sapphire sky.

Her fins were the color,
of plumes of bright peacocks,
that lived on this sapphire beach.

Her sweet maiden song,
flowed over the sand.
To the sapphire stars, it did reach.

The sapphire moon,
and the sapphire sun,
they appeared in twilight together.

And under their glow,
they swam neat and quite slow,
no matter the type of the weather.

These were the maids,
the sea nymphs quite fair,
who lived near this sapphire shore.

And to each maid was thrown,
a stone shining bright,
from the beads sweet *Serenia* wore.

Then under the light,
in the sapphire night,
these maidens swam off in the waves.

And each with a stone,
only mermaids have known,
to be cherished the rest of their days.

#26

The Mermaid *Athena* and the Mariner with the Green Hat

On his head was an old, worn mariner's hat,
and the color of pea green soup.
On his feet were old, worn mariner's boots.
To the shore his shoulders did stoop.

He stood all alone on the shore near his boat,
a skiff with a tattered, old sail.
It needed some work, but the old, sailor had,
not a hammer, nor a rusty old nail.

The seamaid *Athena* was swimming nearby,
in the green-gray waves near the shore.
She saw his sad skiff, and his old, tattered hat.
Up above her, blue seabirds did soar.

With her sweet maiden tune, she called out to these birds,
and whistled a song that they knew.
In a flash they were there, flapping wings in the air,
and making that skiff look brand new.

With their beaks that were strong,
they stitched it together,
as the waves crashed hard on the shore,
and when they were done, this mariner's skiff,
appeared mended and sturdy once more.

Then into the sea, sweet *Athena* did swim,
into waves that were shiny and blue,
while the sailor on shore, just tipped his green hat,
by his skiff that looked shiny and new.

27

The Mermaid *Serafina* and the Silver and Black Sea

A sailor marooned on a pebbled, white beach,
his schooner adrift in the waves,
looked out to the sea, and saw swimming quite free,
a golden-haired, singing seamaid.

Her fins were like ivory, polished, and bright,
her eyes deep blue like the sky.
He called out to her, as the surf, it did surge,
by the beach where this maiden did glide.

So, over the waves *Serafina* did sing,
her lovely and delicate song,
and up from the depths, a whale then arose,
with its tail dark, slashing and long.

She waved to the sailor to swim to the whale,
silver waves rolling off of its back,
and then with a lurch, he was hoisted on board,
in a sea that was silver and black.

Quickly, they rode to his schooner, adrift,
in this sea colored silver and black,
and soon he stood fast at the helm of his ship,
having jumped from the dark whale's back.

His sails unfurled. He looked out to the sea.
Serafina was swimming alone,
and left in the wake of the dark whale's dive,
in the frothy, white, free-flowing foam.

The sailor held fast, then threw from his neck,
as the whale returned to its home,
a necklace of gold from the heart of old Spain,
to a seamaid he barely had known.

28

The Mermaid *Madison* and the Crickets in the Moonlight

Balmy nights on beaches where,
bright lilies grow in fragrant air,
and moonlight soaks lush sandbars where,
tall cattails grow in sea-salt air,
it is here that crickets sing,
in each and every moonbeam path,
where mermaids, with their braids in swaths,
they sing out to their sailor-knights,
the heavens shining, moonbeam-bright.

Sweet *Madison*, a mermaid fair,
with long and flowing scarlet hair,
and eyes as blue as midday skies,
her gentle voice cannot disguise,
her solemn mermaid melody,
a serenade, so lovely.

On beaches covered thick with reeds,
under moonlight flush with weeds,
she sings her sweet and solemn songs,
as crickets sing sweet serenades,
throughout the day and all night long.

And on these beaches, thick with reeds,
throughout the rushes and the weeds,
these serenading crickets sing,
sweet songs the morning light does bring.

Just as these maidens of the sea,
sing out their seamaid melodies,
and in the moonlight's lingering glow,
this lovely music, oh, so low,
soft serenades, they do combine,
with verses soft and ever fine.

And in a ship, its anchor cast,
along this beach where crickets sing,
their music flowing neat and fast,
and over rails, through mizzenmast,
this music reaches to the stern,
and through the crow's nest, ever high,
and underneath a moonlit sky.

The sailors, all, their hands on rails,
hear *Madison's* sweet calming song.
It drifts through mizzenmast and sails,
and in the air it lingers long.

Then from her long hair, she did throw,
as crickets sang in harmony,
white flowers in a ring of gold,
and to a sailor brave and bold.

And in the warm and moonlit air,
this sailor called this mermaid, fair,
and waved her toward his rocking ship,
his finger placed across his lip.

So, in the moon's soft, golden glow,
he threw to her his sailor's hat,
and as she swam so ever slow,
her movement's, sleek, were like a cat's.

Then from her long hair, waving free,
she threw to him white flowers, pure,
as crickets sang along the shore,
just like a kitten's gentle purr.

Then with his red hat, she did swim,
along this beach and to the shore,
looked back toward him upon his ship,
and from his eyes, soft tears did pour.

29

The Mermaid *Adrina* and the Dancing Red Eels

They swirled and they twirled in the soft evening air,
these eels of red, with their dark scarlet stares.
Their colors of red matched *Adrina's* long braids,
and longer than any of the other seamaids,
and they glowed in the darkness like sparkling, red rubies,
as dark and as vibrant as *Adrina's* bright blue beads,
which she wore on her neck, a gift from a sailor,
who sailed the deep seas on a sleek ocean whaler.

In hidden, dark depths below the cold waves,
where eels, they dance in dark and cold caves,
in waters brave mariners seldom do go,
these eels, they swirl, they twirl, and they glow.

These eels as bright as mid-morning suns,
they guard a lost treasure in dark, murky depths,
in waters as silent as voices of nuns,
a treasure that rests in an old pirate's chest.

These bright, crimson eels,
the legend does tell,
will heed the sweet voice,
of a maiden who dwells,
in the cold, deep sea depths,
where these eels do reside,
then swim to far waters,
glowing neat, side by side.

This old mermaid legend,
of these eels that dance,
is known to all maids,
so, she dives, takes a chance,
and below waves where dolphins,
they swim and they play,
in the blue-gray, dark waters,
and under the waves.

30

The Seamaid *Cybele* and the Silver Slippers

Sweet *Cybele,* she sings her song,
across the darting waves,
while angelfish in shoals and shoals,
sleep in the deep sea caves.

But when her siren melody,
does rouse them from their sleep,
they swim to her in swirls and swirls,
below the ocean, deep.

For as the mermaid legend says,
these angelfish in pairs,
will lead a siren princess to,
a cave with fiery flares.

So, sweet *Cybele*, she follows close,
these angelfish so slow,
to lantern fish with colors, bright,
in caves deep down below.

And in one dark and hidden cave,
in waters clear but cold,
these lantern fish with crimson hues,
they flash a fiery glow.

They lead her to a chest of old,
sealed tight with a mermaid's crest,
and in this chest are sliver slippers,
lost on a long sea quest.

These slippers, silver, like an autumn moon,
were worn by a princess maid,
who lived on the shore where a lighthouse stood,
and where this maid did play.

But that was long and long ago,
and now a maid does wait,
and near that lighthouse on the shore,
consigned to her lonely fate.

But then one day from the depths below,
a sea nymph did appear,
and sang to this maid on the sandy shore,
from waters blue and clear.

In her hands were the slippers her mother once
wore,
when this maid was only a child,
and then from a maid of the watery depths,
with a siren of the seas soft smile,
she offered to her these slippers, quite bright,
that glistened and glowed in the dead of the
night.

Cybele then returned to her watery realm,
to a place where the starfish sleep.
Her hair as black as midnight skies,
her eyes were oceans' deep.

This maid on the shore, with a face serene,
wearing bright silver slippers of a maritime
queen,
blew a kiss to this maid from lips so sweet,
bright silver slippers adorning her feet.

31

The Mermaid *Sweet Reese* and the Golden Pearls

The mermaid, *Sweet Reese*,
her hair flowing free,
she swam on her back,
in a greenish-blue sea.

Her fins were the color,
of the pearls that she sought,
golden and bright,
as the legend was taught.

She waited 'til midnight,
and under the moon,
'til it cast its dark shadow,
on a sandy, white dune.

Then onto this dune,
a crow did appear,
and cawed to *Sweet Reese*
when the maiden was near.

Then into the air,
this black bird did fly,
and over the waves,
and over the tides,
then onto a rock,
where the shoreline was steep.
It perched there in silence,
with nary a peep.

The legend she knew,
the mermaid queens told,
a bird of deep black,
it would lead her to gold.

So, she swam to the shore,
where the waters were deep,
and close to a rock,
where the shoreline was steep.

This crow flew away,
as she dove in the waves,
to find golden pearls,
in deep, dark sea caves.

32

The Mermaid *Maraca* and the Pelican with the Red Beak

The mermaid *Maraca*, a maiden quite fair,
has bright, golden fins, and vibrant, red hair.
She swims near an island, where pelicans, they nest,
near a sandbar where's buried a pirate's sea chest.

The legend she follows, a legend of old,
and through all the oceans, this legend is told,
of a reddish-brown pelican with a bright colored beak,
and so this bright bird is the one she does seek.

With a beak of dark red with deep, crimson streaks,
this pelican displays a distinctive bright beak.
He flies near the shore, then roosts on a rock.
In his mouth is a key she knows will unlock,
a chest lost at sea in waves near this beach.
So, to this bright bird, she extends her sweet reach.

This pelican, brown-red, simply nods its bright head,
looks down at blue waves where red crabs, they fed,
then releases this key from its bright crimson beak,
into her sweet hands, with a sea nymph's sweet reach,
as sunlight does dance off this pebbled, white beach,
as the legend of sea nymphs and mermaids did teach.
She then grasps this key, as this bird flies away,
and alights in the sand where a palm tree does sway.

It nods its red head toward the waters nearby,
then over blue waves, this sleek bird does fly.
So, with this gold key in her soft, maiden hands,
the sea nymph *Maraca* swims fast to the sands,
then dives in blue waters in waves that are cold,
to find a lost treasure, like the legend had told.

33

The Mermaid *Cariana*: The Seamaid with the Sapphire Eyes

A sailor adrift in a placid blue sea,
he looked up to the sky,
and what did he see?

He saw lightning and thunder,
and clouds dark as coal,
and then appeared dolphins,
in shoal after shoal,
in the waves 'round his ship,
as rain poured in buckets,
an old whaling hulk,
from the port of Nantucket.

From under dark waves,
a mermaid appeared,
with dolphins in shoals.
The dark skies, they cleared.

This whaler was pushed,
by these sleek and gray fish,
to warm and safe waters,
a sailor's true wish.

Her name, *Cariana*,
a mermaid quite fair,
with bright silver fins,
and bright silver hair,
she glides over waves,
in the soft sea-salt air.

Her eyes are like sapphires,
like fire in the night.
They glow like bright suns,
such a wondrous sight.

She looked at the sailor,
then dove in the waves,
to the hollow, sea depths,
and the dark, hidden caves.

In a flash she was back,
with a golden seashell,
as the dark, flowing sea,
it did rock and did swell.

"In case there is danger,"
she said with a smile.
*"Just blow in the shell,
and then wait for a while."*

"It's magic," she said,
with a glint in her eyes
"An old mermaid legend."
She glanced at the sky.

Then she nodded her head,
like the legend had said,
called back to the dolphins,
the sunset now red,
then returned to the waves,
and the dark, hollow depths,
and the hidden sea caves,
her song sweet on her breath.

34

The Mermaid *Romy* and the Black Heron

As black as darkened skies at dusk,
with eyes as black as onyx pearls,
a heron on a rock ledge rests,
with streaks of gray across its breast,
its beak as orange as fading suns,
its wings as black as robes of nuns.

And in the waters near the shore,
a ship from bold, seafaring lore,
a pirate ship both old and worn,
its sails are dark, black, ripped, and torn.

It lists to aft in rocking seas,
with swabbies on its deck on knees,
and scrubbing old and threadbare wood.
Its captain wears a dark black hood.

No skull-and-crossbones does it fly,
upon its ensign flying high,
that waves in flowing sea-salt breeze,
just a flag that meets the eye,
and black as any midnight sky.

Across its bow, her name is clear,
this pirate ship that sails the seas.
In seaman's script it matched its flag,
above the mizzenmast and frame.
"*Black Heron*" is her sailing name.

The captain of this pirate ship,
a pirate's spyglass on his hip,
his eyes as dark as eyes of sharks,
his face with dark seafaring marks,
his whiskers black as cloud-filled nights,
and to the shore he looked for lights,
to guide him to a passage, swift,
with keys of gold upon his hip.

But through his spyglass in the night,
this lone black heron out of sight,
sweet *Romy* swimming neat and slow,
he only saw, as waves did glow.

And from the glowing on these waves,
sweet *Romy* saw this heron fly,
above the dark and hidden caves,
a slashing, gleaming in its eyes.

And in a flash upon this ship,
its talons black as ancient coal,
as starfish, black, they swam in shoals,
it grasped keys from this captain's hip,
and in the wind its wings did dip,
then flew to where sweet *Romy* swam,
and dropped these keys into her hands.

For as the ancient legend told,
a bird of black would lead to gold,
in waters deep and ever cold,
and sailed by mariners brave and bold.

She follows close this dark, black bird.
A chest of gold these keys will fit.
Below the depths where she will dive,
this dark black bird will be her guide.

OWL

35

The Mermaid *Keysy* and the Crocodile
with the Diamond Eyes

Along a beach in midnight gloom,
where dark black orchids, they do bloom,
there swims a lonely crocodile.
His snout as dark as midnight shadows,
he nestles low in darkened shallows.

The mermaid *Keysy* swims alone,
in waters only she has known,
along this dark and gloomy beach.
Her fins are golden as the sun.
Her hair flows freely when undone.

Her eyes like midnight stars do sparkle,
throughout the dark and gloomy shadows.
She follows close the mermaid legend,
a crocodile asleep in shallows.

This crocodile has eyes like diamonds,
and from the many thousand islands,
flock gannets, gold streaks on their heads.
They land in waters where he fed.

Their eyes are blue like whales' backs,
and point the way to treasures, deep,
just where this crocodile does roam,
in waters where black eels, they sleep.

Along the sandbars they do grow,
blue flag lilies, row by row,
and that is where these gannets land,
in dark but polished pebbled sand.

So, to the gannets she does swim,
and past this crocodile so slow,
to where these gannets beckon her,
above the sea swells, swirling slow.

And there she finds a treasure, lost,
along a sandbar in the gloom,
and where this crocodile swims slowly,
near where the blue flag lilies bloom.

Printed in the United States
by Baker & Taylor Publisher Services